GUPPIES

CONTENTS

Front and back endpapers by Dr. Herbert R. Axelrod.

t.f.h.

ISBN 0-87666-523-7
© 1980 by T.F.H. Publications, Inc.

Distributed in the UNITED STATES by T.F.H. Publications, Inc., 211 West Sylvania Avenue, Neptune City, NJ 07753; in CANADA by H & L Pet Supplies Inc., 27 Kingston Crescent, Kitchener, Ontario N2B 2T6; Rolf C. Hagen Ltd., 3225 Sartelon Street, Montreal 382 Quebec; in ENGLAND by T.F.H. (Great Britain) Ltd., 11 Ormside Way, Holmethorpe Industrial Estate, Redhill, Surrey RH1 2PX; in AUSTRALIA AND THE SOUTH PACIFIC by T.F.H. (Australia) Pty. Ltd., Box 149, Brookvale 2100 N.S.W., Australia; in NEW ZEALAND by Ross Haines & Son, Ltd., 18 Monmouth Street, Grey Lynn, Auckland 2 New Zealand; in SINGAPORE AND MALAYSIA by MPH Distributors Pte., 71-77 Stamford Road, Singapore 0617; in the PHILIPPINES by Bio-Research, 5 Lippay Street, San Lorenzo Village, Makati, Rizal; in SOUTH AFRICA by Multipet Pty. Ltd., 30 Turners Avenue, Durban 4001. Published by T.F.H. Publications Inc., Ltd., the British Crown Colony of Hong Kong. THIS IS THE 1983 EDITION.

GUPPIES

by Wilfred A. Whitern

With a special section on inheritance by Dr. Myron Gordon.

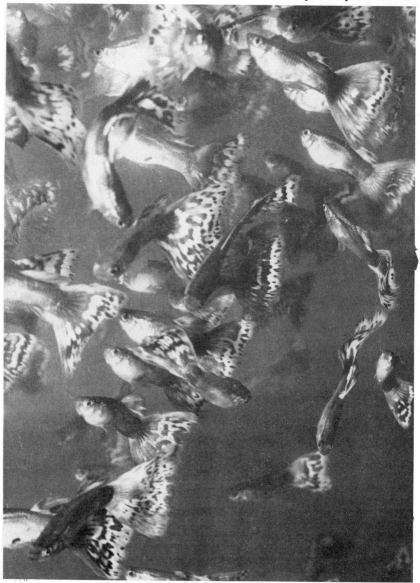

Two of the most difficult characteristics to fix in guppy strains are the color match between the dorsal fin and the caudal fin and the correct shape to the dorsal fin. Photo No. 1 (by Dr. Herbert R. Axelrod) shows a veil-tail male with a good color match between dorsal and caudal fins and excellent shape to the fins. While the other three males (photos by A. Noznov) show a good color match in the fins, they would be faulted on the show bench for poor dorsal fins. The dorsal fin should form a parallelogram, should be about four times as long as wide and should not be twisted.

4

The posterior edge on the caudal fin of the veil-tail guppy to the left is nearly perfect by show standards. Photo by Dr. Herbert R. Axelrod. The ragged points on the caudal fin of the swordtail male below are not desirable show traits. Photo by R. Zukal.

Introduction

Why is the guppy the most popular tropical fish? Many reasons could be advanced explaining the guppy's popularity in terms of its hardiness, beauty, availability, interesting habits and capacity for improvement through genetic experimentation. These things, taken singly, very definitely do account for the popularity of the guppy, but I prefer to believe that they are all small parts of the paramount explanation of this small fish's hold on the aquarium-keeping public. The guppy is the most popular fish because it offers something for everyone. To the beginner looking for a good starter fish and to the casual pet shop browser searching for something that will add a little color to his living room, the

¹ One of the main goals of most guppy breeders is to produce strains that are consistently reproducible. This is often demonstrated in shows by showing guppies of the same sex in groups of two or more. The photos on these two pages show the kind of consistent reproducibility that breeders strive for. These photos were taken by H. Kyselov at a recent guppy competition in Moscow. The red guppies in photo number 1 won first place in the color match class. The male in photo number 2 was one of the third-place winners and the ones in photo number 3 were the second-place winners.

2

3

fish's relatively low price, beauty and hardiness team up to make the guppy the logical candidate for selection. To the advanced hobbyist who has already enjoyed a degree of success in keeping tropical fishes, the guppy throws a challenge: "Here I am," it says. "I'm pretty good already. Can you make me any better?"

It is precisely the acceptance of this challenge that has led to the development of the fancy and super-fancy guppy strains with us today. The original wild guppy was a pleasing fish, but it was far removed from today's brilliantly colored, long-finned specimens. Still and all, it carried within itself the seeds of its current favor, for our present fancy guppy and its forerunner are scientifically identical. Ichthyologists make no distinction between the prize-winning veiltail and the lowliest reject; both are the same fish, *Poecilia reticulata,* and both require the same treatment if they are to be kept successfully. The fancy "hybrid" strains of today are not really hybrids in the strict sense of the word, for they have not been produced through interspecific cross-matings. However, the term "hybrid" has come into popular usage as a means of giving a general classification to the vast body of currently popular varieties.

It cannot be over-emphasized that the present fancy guppies are fish whose beauty cannot be matched, but this should not be the cause for belittling the original wild guppies from which these new strains have been developed. Without the common guppy no advancement would be possible, and there is still ample opportunity for serious aquarists to further improve or develop new color strains.

Long before the present strains of exotic guppies were developed, British and European aquarists were improving, by careful selective breeding, the common wild guppy. From the original wild guppies there appeared over the years such varieties as the speartails, roundtails, cofertails, bottom swordtails, top swordtails, double swordtails, pintails, scarftails and veiltails.

Because this development reached proportions beyond those expected, guppy fancier groups were established. These groups then became a federated group on a national scale, and from this organization there emerged a complete set of guppy standards. From this point on, serious European aquarists tried hard to improve the many strains included within this book of standards. At the same time, American aquarists were not sitting idly by watching their British and European counterparts advance. Paul Hahnel must be given credit for his work in developing the guppy to its present majestic appearance, although many others, such as Alger, Whitney, Sternke and Sweeney, developed individual strains of their own.

Today the emphasis is toward developing larger finnage and more intense and uniformly distributed colors, with the ultimate goal for perfection being the production of a strain in which all fish bear the same color pattern without variation. There still remains an unlimited scope for any aquarist to develop a specialized strain, and it may be presumed that eventually there will appear guppies with a completely solid-colored body and fins of a vivid contrasting color, although some breeders have already come pretty close to that goal.

Undoubtedly the key to the enthusiasm of serious aquarists for the guppy lies in the fact that, irrespective of the great care in selecting a breeding pair, the young from any given mating may vary greatly in their color patterns. Until a strain is fixed, only a small percentage of the fry grow up to resemble their parents exactly. However, these varying color patterns are the foundation upon which further development by experimentation can be undertaken.

Only careful selection of breeding stock will allow successful breeding of guppies. Although uncontrolled, haphazard breeding does occasionally have exciting results, the potential for proper development is greatly diminished.

¹ (1) The ragged caudal fins and poorly formed dorsal fins on these male guppies no doubt cost their owner many show points. Photo by A. Noznov. (2) These blue delta-tail guppies won fifth place in the 1978 Moscow guppy competition. While they are a good color match, their dorsal fins are inadequate. Photo by H. Kyselov.

2

The photo on the left shows the old master, the late Paul Hahnel, standing next to a bank of his guppy tanks. Photo by M.F. Roberts. *Below:* Brazilian guppy breeder Claudio Eduardo Limone inspects a tank of male guppies. Limone is one of the most famous guppy breeders in Brazil. Photo by Dr. Herbert R. Axelrod.

*Equipment
for
Breeding*

16

The first consideration in breeding guppies is the amount of space available. It has often been expressed that guppies can be successfully bred in gallon jars. Although this may be perfectly correct in theory, from the practical viewpoint the limitations of such an operation do not portend any great measure of success, in spite of the fact that guppies will breed under almost any conditions. The most economical approach is to decide to commence operations on a minimum scale, with plans to overcome expansion problems as they may arise.

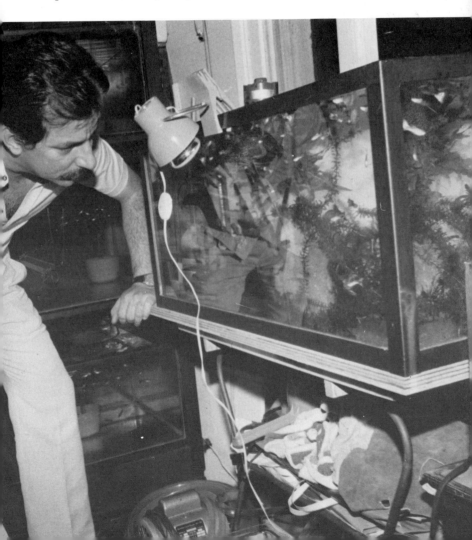

¹ (1) These are the eighth-place winners of the 1978 Moscow guppy competition. They were probably faulted for their poor dorsal fins, that of the upper male being too long and that of the lower male being too short. Photo by H. Kyselov. (2) These were the winners of the first six places in a Singapore guppy show. Photos courtesy of the Singapore Guppy Club.

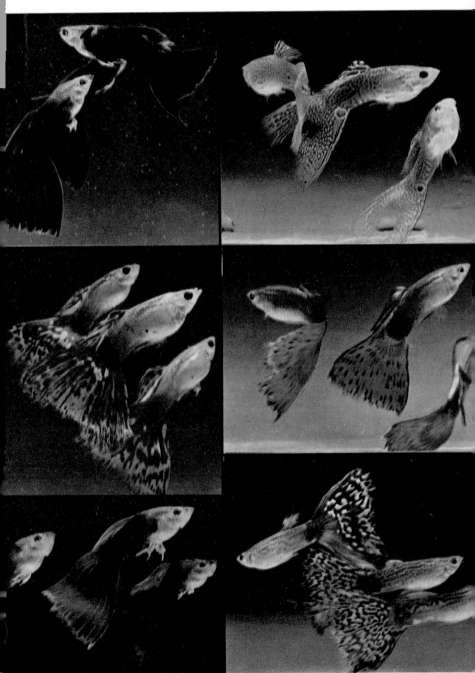

As a reasonable point for commencement, let it be assumed that only one pair of guppies is to be involved. This would require two 5- to 10-gallon aquaria, one for each fish. (It is preferable that for a short period of time the male and female should be maintained separately to permit conditioning.)

Two 15- or 20-gallon aquaria are required for the developing young, one for the males and the other for the females. If the sexes are maintained separately, as they should be, there is afforded the opportunity to bring the young to maturity before attempting to breed them by careful selection.

The beginning guppy breeder should also have several 10-gallon aquaria to be used for the placement of specially selected young once they commence to show their color patterns. Under such an arrangement, special diet experiments may be undertaken. This is a phase of guppy breeding that is often overlooked.

Each tank should be equipped with a filtration and aeration system. Although sub-sand filters are very efficient, the use of outside filters or inside box filters may be preferred, for they can be easily cleaned without disturbing the plant arrangements.

To operate the aeration and filtraton system an air pump is necessary; the pump should have sufficient power to operate the complete system efficiently. Vibrator pumps are easily obtainable, and several of these may be necessary for a large setup. However, piston pumps are more capable of supplying the amount of air required for numerous aquaria.

Aside from the equipment directly concerned with moving the air from pump to tank (tubing, air stones, regulator valves, air filter, etc.), there are other small pieces of equipment that will prove useful. Thermometers, nets, siphoning devices, water testing kits, feeding rings, cleaning pads . . . they all have their uses. The tanks will also need a

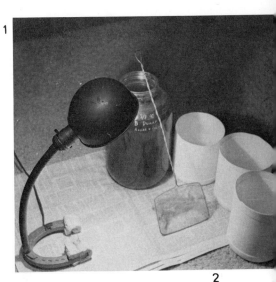

1

(1) Some of the equipment needed for sexing guppies at a very early age. Photo by Fred Howard. (2) A typical setup for rearing large quantities of show guppies. Photo by Dr. Herbert R. Axelrod.

2

lighting system of some sort. These systems come in a variety of styles. There are incandescent bulbs and flourescent bulbs, and several types of housing units for the light. The final choice is up to the individual hobbyist.

It is also advisable to have a large magnifying glass and a small but comprehensive range of medications; these are always available at your local pet store.

A word of caution: whenever purchasing aquaria, equipment or accessories, the cheapest is not always the most economical. If the project, for personal reasons, must be undertaken on a limited budget, start small, but use the best. In the long run there is no substitute for quality.

A dense thicket of water sprite in a guppy show
tank helps the guppies show their colors more vividly. Photo by H. Kyselov. *Below:* Because of its hardiness, *Hygrophila* is a good plant for guppy breeding tanks as well as show tanks. Photo by R. Zukal.

Planting
Arrangements

Plants are an integral part of the good guppy tank, for they are both useful and decorative. They provide shelter, shade and food. Guppies may be maintained without having any plants in their tanks, but such tanks never look as pleasing as planted tanks.

Many aquarists prefer to restrict the compost for their plants to small amounts in ceramic containers in which the plants are grown. However, it is advisable to consider having compost covering the entire bottom of the aquarium. No. 3 gravel is ideal for this purpose, this grade being suffi-

1

(1) *Elodea densa* provides good shelter for females that are being harassed by breeding males. Photo by R. Zukal.
(2) Thickets of floating plants such as *Riccia fluitans* are an asset to the guppy breeding tank, for they provide excellent shelter for baby guppies which head for the surface almost immediately after birth. Photo by Dr. C.D. Sculthorpe.

2

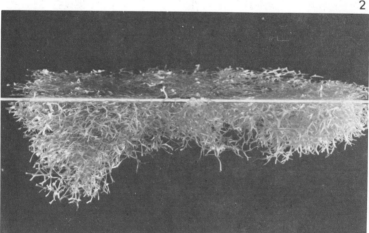

ciently large not to pack too tightly around the plant roots but not large enough to form cavities into which uneaten food may become lodged and foul the water.

The use of natural leaf compost under the gravel is a matter of choice. Many experts feel that it does have a beneficial effect upon the water. If sub-gravel filters are used, these should be covered with about one-half inch of gravel prior to the placement of the leaf compost, and then this should be covered with at least two inches of gravel. When no sub-gravel filters are used, the leaf compost may be placed directly on the bottom and then covered with between two and three inches of gravel. Before being placed in the aquarium, all leaf compost should be baked in the oven at a temperature of around 300 degrees for fifteen minutes. This procedure assures destroying any unwanted parasites or other living pests that might be in the compost. In general, the use of leaf compost is not desirable in the guppy tank.

Choice of plants to be used is more or less a matter of personal taste. Any of the *Sagittaria* or *Vallisneria* varieties are excellent. However, many of the experts prefer to use only watersprite *(Ceratopteris thalicroides)*. They are of the opinion that this plant assists greatly in maintaining the desired water conditions.

In the aquarium in which the females will be placed to deliver their young, it is advisable to have a fairly large mass of floating plants. This can be hornwort *(Ceratophyllum demersum)* or crystalwort *(Riccia fluitans)*. Although there is a difference of opinion regarding whether or not to use breeding traps for gravid females, these should only be introduced where from experience it is known that the female has distinct cannibalistic tendencies towards her young. Experience has proved that well-fed guppies seldom become cannibalistic.

The photo on the left shows a delta-tail green guppy that won first place in its class in a recent German guppy show. Photo by Dr. K. Knaack. Poor water conditions can produce guppies with ragged fins like the ones shown below. Photo by Dr. Herbert R. Axelrod.

Water Conditions

Although it is known that some strains of guppies will withstand above average abuse, particularly in relation to varying water conditions, laxity in their care is not to be considered a desirable practice.

The pH is not critical as long as extremes are avoided. A suitable pH range is 6.6 to 7.6, but once a pH is established it should be maintained as constant as possible. The water hardness (carbonate hardness or the DH) should be around 4 to 6 degrees (approximately 70 to 105 p.p.m.), which is not soft but it is not very hard either.

Although it is possible that the pH may change frequently, but only in very small increments, this should not be considered as being detrimental. The DH will remain fairly constant, provided that the gravel used does not contain soluble salts. Use only natural gravel rather than dolomite or other lime-bearing materials.

Crystal-clear water is not the answer to success, especially when an endeavor is being made to develop one particular color pattern. If a small amount of peat moss is steeped in boiling water, a few drops per gallon of the resultant solution will give the water a slight amber tint. This is a more natural water condition for guppies, and it seems to improve their general physical condition.

Temperature control at a constant level is of some importance, but slight fluctuations that do not vary gradually more than 3 to 5 degrees cause no serious harm to the fish. Temperatures between 72° and 76° F. are ideal.

However, when transferring fish from one aquarium to another, and this is especially important when it involves fry, a careful check must be made to ensure that there is not too much variation in the pH, DH and temperature.

It is an excellent idea that periodically, possibly once a month, a very small amount of common salt should be added to the water. Not more than one-half teaspoonful is required, and about once a month a quarter teaspoonful of pure Epsom salts should be added. These quantities are sufficient for a ten-gallon aquarium; slightly larger doses would be required for larger aquaria. The addition of these two salts, or better yet, a similar amount of a reliable sea salt mix, assists in revitalizing the water by replenishing the salt content that may have been absorbed by the fish, but remember that the addition of any other chemicals to the water should not be undertaken unless there is a positive indicated need. This could be necessary because of disease. Such chemical solutions as are available today do have their specific uses, but they should never be introduced into the

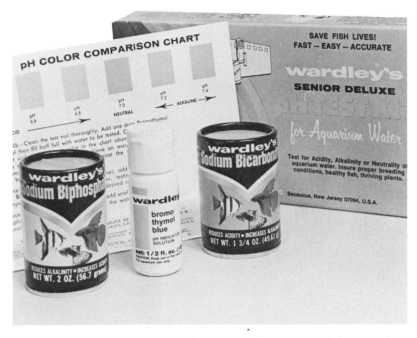

Keeping a check on the pH of the water in the guppy tank is a sensible part of routine aquarium maintenance. Some pH kits contain only the testing agents; others (the kit shown is an example) contain both testing agents and chemicals to adjust the pH of the water.

aquarium water unless absolutely necessary. Of course, adding quantities of chemicals to the water necessitates very frequent partial water changes, which, without the added chemicals, would normally be made only about once every two weeks. Whether partial water changes are being made to dilute medications or as a part of normal routine aquarium maintenance, only about ¼ to ⅓ of the water should be changed at a time and not more than once in 24 hours. Dechlorination is not necessary for a change this small.

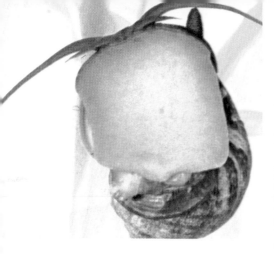

It is important to have scavengers in the guppy rearing tank. Some hobbyists prefer to use the large mystery snails (left) as scavengers. Photo by Dr. Herbert R. Axelrod. *Corydoras* catfishes are frequently raised together with young guppies, for they make excellent scavengers in the guppy tank. Photo by H.J. Richter.

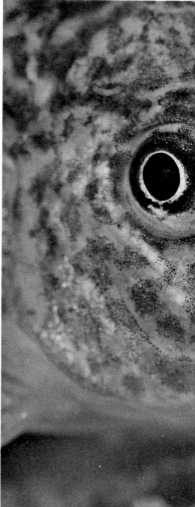

Scavengers

In all aquaria it is only a matter of time before unsightly debris collects on the surface of the gravel. Periodically this accumulation reaches a point where it is necessary to remove it before it causes problems. Aquarium sanitation is very important, because this unwanted debris is the breeding ground for bacterial colonies which are in most instances reponsible for disease.

There are at least two major schools of thought on the use of scavengers in aquaria to prevent the accumulation of organic debris. On the one hand, some hobbyists prefer the

use of snails, for snails will devour any dead matter short of fish feces. They greedily devour uneaten fish food, dead fish carcasses and decomposing plant matter. Furthermore, it can be said with little reservation that snails, at least the types commonly available for use in aquaria, do not eat even very tiny fry.

There are, however, several problems with snails, especially ramshorn snails *(Helisoma* sp.), pond snails *(Lymnaea* sp.) or the hard-shelled *Melanoides* species. They reproduce at such a rapid rate that it is sometimes difficult for aquarists to control their numbers, and if there is not enough organic matter for them to feed upon, they will devour flourishing aquarium plants. Both of these problems can be controlled somewhat, but it does require some extra effort. These snails often show a preference for lettuce leaves over the leaves of aquarium plants. Floating a small piece of lettuce on the surface of the water can supplement their dietary needs sufficiently so as to reduce their predation on aquarium plants. Furthermore, since they tend to accumulate on the lettuce in large numbers, the lettuce can be removed from the tank and discarded, thus keeping the snails' numbers in check.

Most of the problems with snails can be solved through the use of mystery snails *(Ampullaria* sp.), which are quite a bit bigger than those mentioned above. Furthermore, they lay their eggs in masses above the waterline, so the eggs are easy to find and destroy. Some hobbyists also feel that these snails do not destroy flourishing plants as readily as do some of the others.

Another way to prevent snails from destroying plants is to keep the guppies in bare tanks, except for those that one wishes to display. Many hobbyists who are maintaining a large number of aquaria and are producing large numbers of guppies do exactly that. This also helps keep the snails' reproduction in check, for in a bare aquarium the eggs of most species are rather easy to find and destroy.

On the other hand, some hobbyists prefer to use catfish as scavengers in their guppy aquaria. Experience has proved that the best catfishes to use for this purpose are those belonging to the genus *Corydoras.* These peaceful, small catfishes adapt well to a wide variety of aquarium conditions and do not often bother even newborn fry. They constantly dig through the surface gravel, rooting out small bits of food that the other fishes have bypassed. While they readily eat uneaten fish food, they are not as fond of plant debris as are snails. Like snails, and in spite of rumors to the contrary, catfishes are not feces eaters.

Although *Corydoras* catfishes do not usually eat living baby fishes, there have been cases in which such predation has been noticed. Some hobbyists circumvent this problem by breeding the catfishes and raising a few of the catfish fry in each tank right along with the guppy fry. No *Corydoras* will ever bother any living fish that it cannot easily swallow.

Without a doubt, the best way to keep any aquarium from becoming foul due to an accumulation of uneaten fish food is to siphon out the excess following each and every feeding. However, if one has 20 or 30 aquaria in operation, it is not easy to take the time to siphon out each tank every time the fishes are fed, especially since good guppy breeders feed their baby guppies as many as five or six times a day. In that case, it is almost a necessity to have some janitorial help in the way of scavengers living in each aquarium.

It is important to remember that even with catfishes or snails in the aquarium it is occasionally necessary to siphon off any debris that has settled on the bottom. Apart from the unsightly appearance of the debris, it may also be dangerous in relation to the health of both fish and plants.

NUTRAFIN Livebearer Food

For guppies, mollies, and swordtails

NET WT. 1 OZ. (28.4g)

A variety of dry foods should be included in the guppy diet. Some are specially formulated to accommodate the nutritional needs of guppies. *Below:* Healthy guppies usually feed in a frenzy. Even though they have upturned mouths, they are quite capable of feeding from the bottom. Photo by R.A. Stelzer.

*Foods
and
Feeding*

Guppies are not too choosy about foods and are very easily fed. They will accept any dry foods offered; for their size, they have enormous appetites. However, dry food diets are not sufficient and must be augmented with either live, frozen or freeze-dried foods. When in season, collected mosquito larvae make an excellent diet supplement. Tubifex worms are also excellent.

Another useful dietary supplement is the small red garden worm; these should be washed in cold water and finely chopped and can be fed daily. Another raw meat food

that has a high nutritive value is finely scraped frozen raw chicken liver. This is not only greatly enjoyed, but experience has shown that guppies fed liver definitely show more robust growth than those not given this supplementary food. Frozen adult brine shrimp is unquestionably the best frozen food available for guppies.

The basic food for young fry should be newly hatched brine shrimp. After the babies are two months old a twice weekly feeding of white worms should be included in their normal diet.

To raise robust, trophy-winning guppies, it is imperative that young growing specimens be fed as often as possible. It is not uncommon, as mentioned earlier, for a breeder to feed his baby guppies as many as six times a day. In order to do this, one must feed them only small amounts of food at a time. In the long run, it is quite probable that more of the food will wind up as body tissue if the babies are fed in this manner than if one or two larger feedings per day are given. This is the feeding method used by most professional guppy breeders. The same method is also used for conditioning breeders, and it does seem to produce larger broods and a lower mortality rate among the fry.

Not all guppies should be fed this much food. Those that are just past their reproductive prime (about 14 months of age) will tend to become quite obese if they are fed so heavily, and obesity, for many of the same reasons, is as much a problem for fishes as it is for humans. Older guppies should be fed no more than once or twice a day. This will help keep them in prime condition longer, so that they may still be used as show specimens for a while.

While frequent feedings can produce excellent specimens, this is only so if the diet is highly varied. Six feedings a day of one kind of flake food or even one kind of live food such as brine shrimp will not produce superior specimens at all. Rather, it will produce inferior specimens that are more prone to disease, suffering in many different

(1) Brine shrimp is an essential food in the diet of all baby guppies. The eggs of brine shrimp are easy to hatch. (2) Worms can be fed to guppies by using a plastic worm feeder which prevents the worms from spreading all over the aquarium and fouling the water. (3) An assortment of frozen foods should also be included in the guppy diet.

ways from malnutrition and not very prolific. In order to produce good guppies, their diet must be comprised of a great number of different foods. Since no single food contains all of a fish's nutritional needs, a variety of different kinds of foods will ensure that all of their nutritional requirements are met. A good weekly diet should consist of at least two different kinds of dried foods, several different frozen foods (beef heart, clam, fish, beef liver, etc.) or freeze-dried foods and at least one but preferably two different kinds of live foods. Vegetable matter should also be included in the diet. This can be added via green flake foods or by mixing some boiled spinach in with the chopped frozen meats.

Poor nutrition can be one cause of bent spines in guppies. Photo by N.Y.Z.S. Sturdy, disease-free guppies, such as the ones shown below, are not difficult to produce if good aquarium management practices are followed. Photo by R. Zukal.

Diseases

Guppies, like all other fishes, are prone to disease, and although an ounce of prevention is worth a pound of cure, there are times when it is better to destroy a diseased fish than attempt to effect a cure.

All diseases have an origin, but some are hereditary and usually are beyond the scope of fish disease treatment. Many diseases are caused because of a lack of proper aquarium management. Lack of understanding of the fundamentals required for good aquarium management is the basic reason for the majority of common disease outbreaks in the guppy aquarium. It has been mentioned that a good

diet, steady environmental conditions and frequent partial water changes are paramount to good aquarium management. The water changes can virtually eliminate outbreaks of many common fish diseases such as ich, velvet and fin rot. Healthy fishes are capable of resisting these diseases, but fishes that are in poor overall health or are being kept in a stressed or incorrect environment are not very resistant to these diseases. Frequent water changing helps dilute organic pollutants in the water that arise from fish and plant wastes, thus keeping the concentration of these pollutants below a level that can affect the fish and below the level that encourages the proliferation of many disease organisms.

Many fine guppies can be cured of a disease if all the necessary equipment and medications are immediately available. Delay can allow the disease to spread to such proportions that a normally therapeutic dose of the chosen medication may not be effective. However, it is never advisable to try to hurry a cure for any disease; many diseases have a specific time cycle, and the application of additional medication beyond the recommended dosage will not hasten the cure. Furthermore, it can be dangerous to use larger than prescribed doses of any given medication. Many of them contain ingredients that are harmless to the fish if used as prescribed, but dosages in excess of the prescribed amount can sometimes be lethal. The same idea usually applies to the use of two or more medications at one time. Their effects can sometimes nullify each other or they can act synergistically, often to the detriment of the fish. In other words, drugs can have effects when used together that they don't have when used separately, effects which can be lethal to fishes.

Never gamble with a disease, especially if you've just spent a year or two developing a new strain of guppy or improving an old strain. If the disease strikes in an aquarium and is contagious, remove all the fish immediately and place them in isolation, separating those that already have visible signs of the disease into one tank and those that are still free of the symptoms into another tank. The aquarium should then be stripped down. The sand or gravel should be sterilized in a strong saline solution for about 24 hours, then thoroughly rinsed. Commercial sterilizing solutions such as methylene blue are available in pet shops. Plastic plants, heaters, thermometers and virtually all non-organic materials can be left in the tank for sterilization, but be advised that some commercial disinfectants permanently discolor gravel, rocks, plastic plants and other equipment. As another alternative, the gravel can be removed and boiled in water, but the tank and the rest of its contents must still be sterilized. *Do not use hot water in an aquarium,* as it will crack the glass. Live plants can be sterilized by soaking them no longer than five minutes in a solution of alum, a product available from most pharmacies. Mix a teaspoon of alum to each quart of room-temperature water used. The plants should be rinsed thoroughly after a five-minute soak.

It should be remembered that many disease organisms are present even in healthy aquaria and that these organisms will only proliferate when conditions are right for them. A weak or stressed fish is an open invitation to an outbreak of disease. When a fish is under stress of any kind, its reaction is to lose some of its body slime. Under normal conditions a fish's body slime protects it from infection by many different disease organisms, but when the coating of slime becomes thinner than normal or is cast off altogether, the fish is very susceptible to these diseases. Environmental stress is therefore one of the primary causes of disease.

CHEMICAL POISONING

General symptoms of environmental upset should be recognized by the aquarist in order to head off diseases before they break out. If a guppy hangs at the surface gasping for air, this is a sure sign that the water has become low in oxygen. This is usually due to excessive organic decomposition in the aquarium. Uneaten foods and dead fish, snails and plants can trigger this condition. Organic decomposition consumes oxygen in the water and increases the amount of dissolved carbon dioxide, thus the fishes are being asphyxiated. This can be rectified by making a partial water change, removing the source of pollution and by temporarily increasing the strength of aeration.

Ammonia poisoning is another result of excessive decomposition. Guppies may rub themselves on objects in the aquarium, shake their heads and breathe very rapidly and heavily. Oxygen depletion and carbon dioxide poisoning complicate the situation, because under those conditions fishes are much more sensitive to even minute amounts of ammonia in the water. The cure is the same as it is for carbon dioxide poisoning and oxygen insufficiency. However, if the amount of ammonia is so great that a water change and heavy aeration don't help (sometimes a water change can make the problem worse), then it may be necessary to temporarily lower the pH of the water just a bit. A few drops of household vinegar or an appropriate amount of sodium biphosphate will do the job. Lowering the pH renders the ammonia harmless. The lowering should be done gradually, however, because a sudden drop in pH can be as stressful to a fish as a sudden drop of temperature. Furthermore, if there is an excess of carbon dioxide present, lowering the pH will make that situation worse. A temporary gradual drop in pH to about 6.6 will not permanently harm most guppies as long as the source of the pollution is removed and the pH is gradually brought back up to about neutral after a few days.

Another complication caused by excessive organic decomposition in the aquarium is acidosis. This results from prolonged exposure to extremely acidic conditions which are usually caused by heavy organic decomposition.

Fishes suffering from acidosis may show hemorrhagic marks on the skin, especially at the fin bases and around the eyes, nostrils and lips. They show rapid and heavy breathing. They lie about the bottom of the tank and may suddenly, on the slightest provocation, begin to madly dash about the aquarium, colliding with everything in sight including each other, coming to rest once again on the bottom of the tank or in the fork of a plant, with almost no signs at all of breathing.

The symptoms of acidosis call for immediate and drastic action. Almost a complete water change is necessary. The pH must be returned to normal in this case *rather quickly.* Immediate and total withdrawal from feeding is necessary. Normal aeration should be continued, and the tank should be completely darkened for a few days by covering the sides and top with black paper. After a few days the paper can be gradually withdrawn and feeding gradually restored, but all will be to no avail if the source of the pollution is not found and eliminated.

DROPSY

Dropsy itself is not a disease. Rather, it is a sign of various diseases in which the abdominal cavity fills with fluid. Internal bacterial infection is usually the cause of the condition. A dropsical fish has a swollen abdomen and its scales are raised at an angle to the body. Until recently, more often than not dropsy was not a curable condition. It was realized that dropsy was an internal infection and that medications should be given to the fish internally, but methods of introducing medications into fishes were not commonly known until recently. Hobbyists, therefore, depended upon standard medications being absorbed through the skin of the fish. This, of course, does not happen with most commercially available aquarium remedies. There are now, however, several products on the market that can be absorbed into an ailing fish's internal systems through both the skin and the gills. Among them, the furan derivatives are especially effective in treating internal bacterial infections. Standard aquarium antibiotics can be used to treat dropsy if they are put into the fish's food so that they are taken internally. For this method of treatment to be effective, it requires that the aquarist recognize the signs of internal bacterial infection in its very early stages so the guppy can be medicated before it loses its appetite. It is suggested that the medicated food be given to other guppies in the tank that are not yet showing signs of the disease. This should effectively prevent the spread of an infectious internal bacterial disease in the aquarium.

There are other kinds of dropsical conditions that are not contagious, and there are still many causes of dropsy that are not curable. If the properly treated fish does not respond positively within a few days, it should be destroyed and properly disposed of.

A constipated or egg-bound female guppy is often mistakenly treated for dropsy. In either case the abdomen can become severely swollen, but the scales usually do not stand off the body. Both of the latter conditions can usually be rectified by dietary modification. It may be necessary to help a bound up female pass dead eggs and accumulated fecal matter by holding her in a wet net and gently massaging the body from the front toward the rear and down toward the vent.

POPEYE

Exophthalmos or popeye is one of the symptoms of diseases such as *Ichthyophonus* (also called *Ichthyosporidium*), which is an internal fungal disease, bacterial kidney disease and piscine tuberculosis. In popeye, pockets of fluid and sometimes gas build up behind the eyes, thus causing the eyes to bulge outward.

Bacterial kidney disease and piscine tuberculosis can be treated by including wide-spectrum antibiotics in the infected fish's food, but the treatment only occasionally cures the disease. Non-infected guppies from the same tank should be treated in the same way to prevent the infection from spreading.

If popeye is caused by *Ichthyophonus,* small white areas will develop on the skin of the infected fish at a later stage of the disease. The disease is not curable, but it is preventable by maintaining immaculately clean aquarium conditions. Infected fishes should be destroyed and disposed of.

WHITE SPOT DISEASE (ICH)

There are few aquarists who have not had some experience with this highly contagious disease. Ich or white spot disease is caused by a protozoan called *Ichthyophthirius multifiliis.* Ich parasites are present in nearly every aquarium, but they remain dormant if the fishes in the tank remain unstressed. However, when stress occurs, especially the stress caused by a sudden drop in temperature of more than just a few degrees, guppies become highly susceptible to attacks by this disease.

One of the earliest signs of ich is guppies rubbing themselves on objects in the aquarium. After a few days, white spots about the size of grains of salt begin to appear all over the infected fish. The white spots are individual parasites that have imbedded themselves in the victim's skin, fed on the host's body fluids for a few days and have become encysted. After a day or two the cysts start to drop off the host, but others are at the same time just beginning to form. The cysts drop to the bottom of the tank and the protozoan within begins to multiply by division. Finally, after a day or two the cyst breaks open, releasing as many as 500 new free-swimming ciliated parasites, each immediately seeking a host. Familiarity with the life cycle of this parasite makes it easy to understand why this disease spreads so rapidly among aquarium fishes and also helps one understand how to treat the disease.

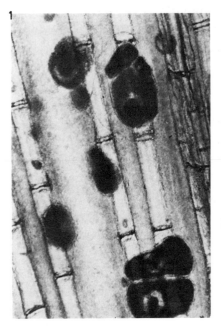

(1) A microscopic view of an ich-infested fin. (2) Ich looks like grains of salt sprinkled on a fish's fin or body. Photos by Dr. G. Schubert.

The only stage in the life cycle of ich in which it is vulnerable to standard treatment is the free-swimming stage. This stage rarely lasts more than 24 hours, but treatment must be continued for no less than 10 days to catch all of the parasites in this stage.

There are ways to cure this disease without using chemicals. It has been discovered that the free-swimming ich parasites cannot survive very long in water that is heated to 86° F. This temperature will not harm the fishes for the necessary 10 days if heavy aeration is maintained. The extra aeration is necessary because at warmer temperatures water holds less dissolved oxygen than it does at cooler temperatures. If the disease is caught in its early stages heat treatment should stop it. A tablespoon of non-iodized salt added to each gallon of water seems to have some effect in stopping the disease when the heat treatment is used. Rather than killing the parasites themselves, the addition of salt may help the fishes be more resistant to further attack.

In eradicating the disease from the aquarium, extra assurance that the parasites are either gone or returned to a dormant stage can be had by removing all fishes from the aquarium for two to three weeks. Without the availability of hosts the free-swimming parasites will die of starvation. The remaining unattached cysts go into a dormant state and remain there as long as the fishes remain healthy.

For more severe cases of ich, the disease can be treated with a chemical called malachite green. This chemical is available under a number of different trade names and is often mixed in commercial preparations with a wide assortment of other helpful chemicals.

VELVET

Velvet disease is caused by another protozoan called *Oodinium*. The cysts show up on the body of the fish as a velvety golden coating. They are much smaller than the cysts of ich, and accordingly they are much more difficult to detect. The initial symptoms are about the same as those of ich but usually are not as severe. The life cycle of the parasite is about the same as that of ich, but the treatment is a bit different. *Oodinium* parasites do not respond to heat treatment as readily as ich parasites do, and the chemical of choice is acriflavine rather than malachite green. The treatment should be continued for 10 to 15 days so as to kill all free-swimming parasites.

FIN ROT

Fin rot is probably the second most frequent disease observed by aquarists and is one that can cause great losses if not given immediate attention. The disease usually commences in the caudal fin and rapidly spreads to other fins. The first visual sign of the disease is that the caudal fin becomes ragged along the posterior edge. Shortly after the fins take on the ragged appearance a white edging appears along the ragged margins. Initially fin rot is usually caused

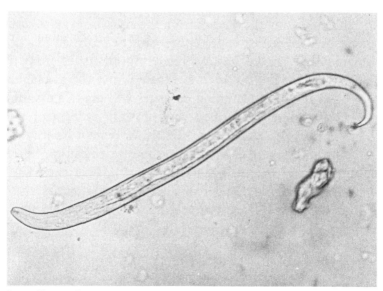

Camallanus is a nematode worm that very commonly attacks livebearers such as guppies and swordtails. The worm has a reddish color and is often seen protruding from the anus of an infected fish. Post-mortem examinations of these fishes have revealed hundreds of the worms in the visceral cavity. Trichlorfon, a well-known cattle insecticide, can be used to treat guppies having *Camallanus* infestations. Photo by Dr. G. Schubert.

by an external bacterial infection, and it can be effectively treated by dissolving a wide-spectrum antibiotic such as Tetracycline® in the water. The treatment should be carried out in an isolation tank since wide-spectrum antibiotics also kill the beneficial bacteria in the biofilter.

A secondary development with fin rot is the attack of dead fin tissue by fungi such as *Saprolegnia*. If the disease is not stopped quickly, the fungus spreads to other areas of the body including the mouth. This type of fungus is highly contagious. Other types of fungi also attack the body and the mouth. Fungal hyphae can be noticed on the diseased fish as a cottony growth. In addition to continuing the antibiotic treatment, fishes infected with fungus should be removed from the water and held in a wet net while the infected area is swabbed with Mercurochrome® .

WORMS AND OTHER PARASITES

There are several kinds of worms that attack aquarium fishes, but one of particular concern to guppy enthusiasts is the intestinal roundworm or nematode called *Camallanus*. *Camallanus* does attack other fishes, but it is most frequently reported in livebearers. It is a red- or orange-colored worm that lives in the intestine of its hosts and feeds from its host's blood and other body fluids. The worm is first noticed protruding from the anus of its host.

Camallanus is transmitted to aquarium fishes by *Cyclops,* which are unfortunately one of the favorite foods of guppies and are eaten by them in large quantities in the wild. *Cyclops* sometimes find their way into farm ponds, which is how domesticated strains of guppies become infected.

The most effective treatment for a *Camallanus* infestation is a chemical whose generic name is trichlorfon. It is an insecticide used by cattle farmers and wildlife managers. It is sold under the trade name of Dylox® as well as under three or four other popular names, and it is usually carried in veterinary supply stores or farm supply stores. Unfortunately, it is not usually sold in quantities sufficiently small for the treatment of a few fishes, so its use is only practical for the large-scale breeder. For the hobbyist with a few tanks of guppies, there are several commercial products that are useful in treating a variety of intestinal worms including *Camallanus*.

Another parasite frequently encountered by guppy enthusiasts is the anchor worm, *Lernaea cyprinacea*. It is not actually a worm but is a modified form of a parasitic copepod. It can also be eradicated with trichlorfon.

Two male guppies should never be kept with only one female, as they will harass the female constantly. Photo by R. Zukal. Half-black delta-tail guppies are frequently available in tropical fish shops and are a good strain for beginning guppy breeders. Photo by Dr. Herbert R. Axelrod.

Selecting Breeding Stock

To attempt to improve an existing strain or eventually develop a new strain, it is vitally essential that in selecting the breeding stock only the best should be obtained.

Because guppies are such prolific breeders, it is very unwise to commence with several pairs. Such an undertaking demands additional equipment and room which may not be available. Selecting one pair with the color characteristics that appeal to you is the best plan. This pair should be young enough to ensure that they have not been bred previously.

In making the selection the fish should be closely examined, taking particular care that the body formation is sturdy, well developed and of good shape. In the males it is wise to select a fish that has the color characteristics you desire, but the greatly enlarged caudal fin should not be of such proportions as to cause the fish to swim unnaturally.

The female should be nearly twice as large as the male, and she should have a sturdy, well-rounded body with good depth. Particular attention should be given to any color patches or other markings she may have, because this may assist in producing a better color pattern in the offspring.

Guppies are well known for color variations, and this is especially evident when breeding fancy guppies. It should not be expected that when bred the offspring will closely resemble the parents. It is more than probable that only between 40 and 50% will have the same colors and markings.

Female guppies should be selected for their sturdy appearance as well as good coloration. Even though this young female appears to be a good specimen, she should not be selected, for she is old enough to have been fertilized and may be past her breeding prime by the time she has used all of the sperm from her first fertilization. Photo by R. Zukal.

This male veil-tail guppy has a well-formed caudal fin. The fin should spread from the peduncle to an angle of about 45 degrees and should be about the same length as the body. A guppy breeder would strive to produce a straighter posterior edge on the caudal fin than this male has. Photo by Dr. Herbert R. Axelrod.

However, there may be more striking patterns with more vivid colors in the young fry that do not resemble the parents.

It is from this stock that there is provision for development, but this will not be accomplished in a short time. Patience and a willingness to take disappointment are the price that must be paid.

The numerous fine vivid color patterns available today have taken many years to produce. However, the limit has not been reached, and there is ample room for any serious aquarists to still further improve on the "hybrid" guppy.

The basic principle involved and to be remembered is that you cannot expect to develop outstanding strains of guppies by commencing with poor stock. Of course, such stock could eventually be developed and improved upon, but the time needed would be wasted when it is so easy to get breeding stock of high quality.

The male guppy usually approaches the female from above and behind for fertilization. Photo by the American Museum of Natural History. *Below:* Baby guppies are usually born headfirst. Photo by M. Chvojka.

Breeding Guppies

For the initial endeavor, it is essential that the female selected be of virgin stock and not more than three months old. The male should be of approximately the same age.

This pair should be maintained in separate aquaria and placed on a feeding schedule of conditioning foods. These include daily feedings of live or frozen foods such as *Daphnia*, mosquito larvae, brine shrimp and white worms. This type of food should be augmented daily with a dry food of high quality.

As these young fish mature they should be closely observed for any outstanding color markings. When the pair is around six months old, they should then be placed into an aquarium together. Once the female displays the darkening of the gravid spot it is safe to assume that young are on the way. As this gravid spot deepens and moves slightly downward toward the vent, delivery is not far away. The female should be placed in a separate aquarium, not necessarily in a breeding trap. Large masses of floating plants are all that is needed.

Once the first batch of young has appeared, remove the female to a separate aquarium. The newly delivered fry should remain in the aquarium for at least one week. Daily close observation should be kept and young fish showing deformities should be removed and destroyed or fed to larger fish.

Scarf-tail guppies are a good strain for beginning guppy breeders, for they are usually hardy fish. A consistently reproducible strain such as this one is usually a good one with which to begin breeding guppies. Photo by R. Zukal.

The male guppy thrusts the gonopodium (arrow) forward to inject sperm into the female. Photo by the American Museum of Natural History.

After they are one week old the sex differences can be observed, but it will require the assistance of a large magnifying glass.

Sexing of the fry is not a difficult procedure if the following system is used: Acquire a two-gallon aquarium and cover the back with a black card that has a half-inch round hole in the center. Attach this card to the front of the aquarium, with the black facing the inside. Behind the hole place a small lamp containing a 100-watt frosted bulb. Fill the aquarium with water from the aquarium containing the fry to be sexed. Place two or three of the fry in this specially prepared aquarium; with the help of a three-inch magnifying glass it is very easy to distinguish the sexes. As each little fish passes through the beam of light the gravid spot of the females can easily be seen. Greater success will be achieved if this is undertaken in the evening in a darkened room.

After one month to six weeks, any of the fry displaying unusual color designs that are different from that of the parents should be segregated into another smaller aquarium of approximately ten gallons capacity. This procedure should also be followed as far as the females are concerned. Any that show a slight body coloration or spots or splashes of color on the fins should be treated in this manner.

When the females have reached an age of six months, select one or two that have well shaped bodies and excellent finnage and place these in the aquarium containing their father.

For the more serious aquarist whose main desire is to develop and sustain a specialized color strain (and this may take several years of careful selective breeding), there is a method by which the color a female will transmit to her young may be discovered. This is known as the "hormone test," and the procedures for such a test are very simple. Obtain a solution of 0.1 gram of methyl testosterone in 100 cc. of 70% methyl or ethyl alcohol. To this solution add 900 cc. of distilled water. This will comprise your stock solution for making the tests. It is very important that only two drops of this solution per gallon of water be used. Any overdose of this solution can have a serious effect upon the females tested, to the point where they may be sterilized. From a safety viewpoint, it is best if the water to be used for this test be measured carefully by using a standard gallon measuring can. Five gallons of water would require ten drops of the solution.

The females to be tested should be placed in a newly set-up aquarium, which should contain no gravel or plants. The time required for the test to develop is from two to six weeks. The test will cause the females to color-up to that color they will eventually transmit to their male offspring. Once the females have developed their color, select the one having the desirable qualities in which you are interested. Allow another month for the effects of the test to wear off, although in some instances some females never return to their normal color pattern. After this period has elapsed the selected female may be placed with the selected male.

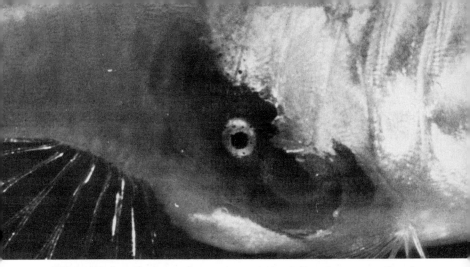

When the female guppy is nearly ready to deliver her young the abdominal wall is usually stretched quite a bit, making it easy to see the developing young in the abdominal cavity. Photo by Ralph Guillumette.

If you have room for the additional equipment, several males and females of the first batch of young may be bred. However, it is important that each batch of young from such matings be developed in individual aquaria and not be mixed with other broods of young. It is only in this manner, and with strict adherence to every phase of the development, that improvement in the color strain or development of a new color pattern can be achieved successfully.

The in-breeding of fancy guppies has no limits, and the acquisition of new stock from sources other than where the original stock was purchased will provide new channels for endeavor. Never refuse an opportunity to acquire stock that may be larger or more colorful than your own. By cross-breeding these new strains with your own stock there is always the potential of developing an entirely new and beautiful "hybrid" guppy. These transformations are not acquired in one breeding. They demand not only patience and keen observation but also much time spent on long and tedious experiments that will have many disappointments along the way.

An assortment of shapes can be bred into the fins of swordtail guppies. Photo by M.F. Roberts. The veil-tail guppies below have caudal fins that are too short for show specimens. By selective breeding, the tails can be properly lengthened. Photo by Dr. Herbert R. Axelrod.

Inheritance in the Guppy

The key to the scientific breeding of animals including fishes may be found in the principles of inheritance. These were discovered by Gregor Mendel over one hundred years ago, and although Mendel revealed his principle of inheritance from his study of pea plants, the same principles apply to most plants and to animals, too. One of the best examples of these principles may be illustrated by the inheritance of the golden coloration in the guppy. Dr. H.B. Goodrich and his associates at Wesleyan University in Connecticut worked this problem out first, and then their work was confirmed in all details by Doctors Caryl P. and Edna

F. Haskins of the Haskins Laboratory in New York City. They discovered that 1. when a golden guppy male is mated to an ordinary gray female, or 2. when a golden guppy female is mated to an ordinary (non-golden) male, 3. only ordinary gray daughters and gray sons are produced. These are called the members of the first filial generation, which is often abbreviated to read: F_1. When any pair of guppies of the first or F_1 generation are mated brother to sister, each pair will produce on the average three gray offspring to one golden in the second filial generation.

If this simple experiment is clearly understood, many false notions concerning inheritance will be cleared up. Of course, this is not all there is to know about the science of heredity or genetics, but it is the beginning, the first step forward to a mastery of the methods every breeder may apply to improve his favorite strain of guppies. See the accompanying chart and study the following method in predicting the results of a mating between parents that differ in one inherited trait such as gold coloring.

Golden Female	Ordinary Male
gg	GG

1. Let the golden guppy female be represented by two small g's, because *golden*, as we will see, is recessive to the ordinary *gray* coloring.

2. Let the *gray* colored male be represented by two capital G's, because *gray* is dominant to *golden*.
First Generation (F_1) will be:

Gray Daughters	Gray Sons
Gg	Gg

Note that the constitution of the gray offspring of the first generation (F_1) is *Gg*, meaning that they carry one recessive *(g)* and one dominant *(G)* hereditary factor or gene for the trait in question. In spite of the fact that they are *Gg*, they look like *GG;* that is, both are *gray*. This is because *G* is dominant to *g*. This means in genetic terms that *gray* is dominant to *golden*.

Inheritance of Albinism in the Guppy

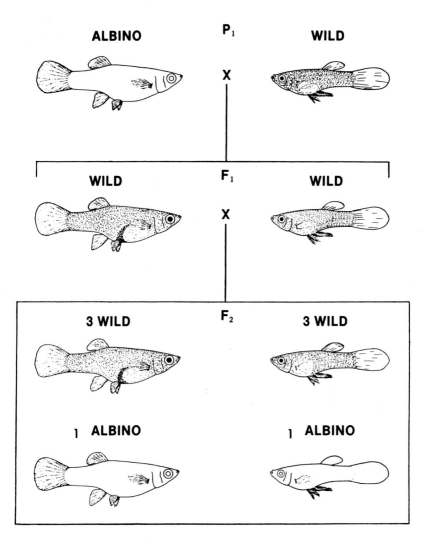

An albino guppy when mated with a wild type (P₁) produced all wild type offspring in the first generation (F₁). From this mating, if two wild type individuals are bred brother to sister, they theoretically should produce in the second generation (F₂) three times as many wild type offspring as albinos. This chart represents an ideal experiment. The actual results rarely produce an exact 3 to 1 ratio.

Now when two gray guppies of the first generation (F_1) are bred brother to sister, Gg x Gg, the following recombinations of their various hereditary possibilities will result:

Each egg or ovum produced by the F_1 guppy sister, Gg, will contain either one or the other color gene.

Each sperm or spermatozoan produced by the F_1 guppy brother, Gg will also contain either a G or g gene.

How G and g genes may combine to produce the color types in the F_2 may be expressed in a Punnett square as follows:

Ova from F_1 Gray Female

		G	g
Sperm from F_1 Gray Male	G	1. GG Gray	3. Gg Gray
	g	2. Gg Gray	4. gg Golden

Since items No. 1, 2 and 3 within the squares GG, Gg, and Gg are gray, these represent 3 gray F_2 Guppies. Item No. 4, gg, represents a Golden Guppy. Thus the typical Mendelian ratio of 3 grays to 1 golden is demonstrated in the members of the F_2 generation.

THE WILD TYPE OF GUPPY

The skin of the gray female guppy, when observed under the microscope, contains hundreds of small black pigment cells or melanophores. The word "melanophore" is derived from *melanin*, a black, chemically stable substance, and *ophorus*, to carry. Thus, a melanophore is a melanin particle-carrying cell. The melanophore has certain special physiological properties. The melanin particles in a melanophore may be dispersed throughout the cell, or the pigment particles may be grouped in a small area in the center of the cell. Whether the particles are dispersed or concen-

The male in the lower right corner of this photo is a rarely seen lyretail guppy. By its appearance it seems to be a derivative of the scarf-tail, the strain shown above it. However, it could be derived independently of the scarf-tail. Notice its similarity to the double swordtail male. Photo by M.F. Roberts.

trated in the melanophore depends upon the physiological state of the animal. For example, if a fish hovers over a white sandy bottom, its body becomes pale and matches its background. In this case the pigment granules are concentrated in the centers of the melanophores. If the fish moves directly over dark rocks or black mud, its eyes act as a sensory pick-up and this initiates a chain reaction through a series of nerves that brings about a dispersal of melanin particles in the melanophores. As a consequence, the fish becomes darkly colored. We know that the eyes are vital in starting the reaction because, if blinded accidentally or in the course of experimentation, the fishes cannot make the pigmentary readjustments to their background. The melanophores remain in an in-between state.

5 6

The swordtail trait in guppies has been produced in several different forms and in combination with numerous body colors. (1) A double swordtail Viennese emerald. (2) A double swordtail gold. (3) A lower swordtail emerald. (4) A lower swordtail gray. Photos 1, 2, 3 and 4 by Dr. K. Knaack. (5) A top swordtail guppy. Photo by E. Schmidt. (6) The form of this double swordtail is nearly perfect, but the dorsal fin should be just a bit longer by IFGA standards. Photo by W. Foersch.

THE GOLDEN GUPPY

If one could remove the hundreds of tiny melanophores that are ordinarily present in a wild gray female guppy, or if one could by some chemical process reduce the numbers of black pigment granules radically, one would produce a golden variety. We know of no chemical that will do this, without killing the guppy in the process, but one chance hereditary change or *mutant* did the trick. The *golden (g)* mutant reduced the number of melanophores by about fifty per cent. When the number of black pigment cells in the skin of the guppy were reduced to half, the yellow pigment cells which were always present there were uncovered. Curiously, the melanophores that remained in the golden guppy are slightly larger than the usual type, but being relatively few they are unable to hide the underlying yellow coloration. The yellow color of the golden guppy is made possible by many yellow-colored cells that contain a xanthine-like substance.

When the Wesleyan University geneticists mated a wild-type guppy with a golden one, they obtained 257 first gen-

Melanophore Density in Various Guppy Strains

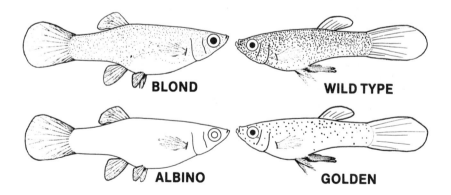

BLOND

WILD TYPE

ALBINO

GOLDEN

Various color strains of guppies interbreed freely. This is one reason that the serious guppy breeder isolates the fish by sex at as early an age as possible. Photo by Dr. K. Knaack.

eration (F_1) offspring, all of which were gray colored like their wild parent. When they mated two of the gray F_1 guppies together, brother to sister, they obtained 230 gray to 74 golden guppies among the members of the second generation (F_2).

The results convinced the experimentalists that *golden* was a simple Mendelian recessive and the reader will agree with them if he wishes to make a few calculations. This may be done by counting all the fish obtained in the second generation; there were 230 grays and 74 goldens, which adds up to 304. Assume that the ideal ratio of 3 to 1 should be attained in the second generation population when the mating was accomplished as indicated previously. Then, on the basis of 304 individuals, there should have been 228 grays and 76 goldens. When compared with the theoretical numbers of grays and goldens expected (228 to 76), the actual results obtained (230 to 74) are remarkably close.

(1) In matched pair competition, guppy breeders strive to have both sexes colored as much alike as possible. Although the pattern is similar in this male and female, the colors are too different for this pair to score many points. Photo by A. Noznov. Photos 2 through 5 show various color forms being bred into female guppies. Photos 2 and 3 by Midge Hill. Photo 4 by Dr. S. Frank. Photo 5 by V. Dazkewitsch.

3

4

5

THE BLOND GUPPY

Professor H.B. Goodrich of Wesleyan University had another and lighter strain of golden-like guppies which he called *blond*. Placed under the microscope, the blond guppy's skin showed just about as many melanophores as that of the wild gray guppy, but the black pigment cells were extremely small and dot-like. Apparently the melanophores of the blond are unable to disperse their melanin particles to the degree that normal black pigment cells can. Thus the guppies that have the blond mutant appear golden in color—indeed the blonds are much lighter and more translucent than golden guppies. This is a beautiful example of how two distinct mutations, one *gg*, the other *bb*, produce two different reactions, yet in external appearance the blond and golden guppies resemble each other.

When the blond guppy was mated to the wild gray in one series of experimental crosses, all their first generation off-

Except for the irregular posterior edge, this male veil-tail guppy shows an almost perfect caudal fin. The angle of the edges of the fin should be 40 to 50 degrees. Photo by R. Zukal.

The male guppies in this photo are scarf-tails. These are often confused with veil-tails by the novice guppy keeper. Notice that the upper and lower edges of the caudal fins of these males are nearly parallel. This is a definite scarf-tail trait. Photo by M.F. Roberts.

spring (F_1), of which there were 77, were *gray*. When the first generation (F_1) gray guppies were mated brother to sister, a total of 285 second generation (F_2) guppies was obtained, of which 224 were *gray* and 61 were *blond*. On the basis of the 3 to 1 ratio expected in the F_2 members, there should have been 214 wilds to 71 blonds. Doctor Goodrich believed that the blond guppies were not as strong as the wild type. This differential viability could account for the small discrepancies between the expected numbers of the two color types and the numbers the doctor actually obtained in the F_2 members. These results are very much like those obtained in an F_2 population from an original mating of the golden platy to the wild gray platy. Not as many golden platies were obtained in the second generation as expected on the basis of the 3:1 ratio. Although blond guppies are weaker than gray ones, blond guppies are considerably stronger than albino guppies.

1   2

3

4

The birth process shown in two different female guppies. (1) The baby begins to emerge from the genital opening. (2) The young usually emerge from the mother head-first or in a curled position. (3) The fry immediately uncurl after they are ejected from the vent. (4) The baby's first "trip" after it uncurls is usually to the surface where the swim bladder is filled with air for the first time. Photos by R. Zukal.

THE ALBINO GUPPY

The albino guppy appeared during the early 1940's in the in-bred stocks of the late physician Dr. Abbs of Ampere, New Jersey, whose avocation was breeding superior guppies.

Dr. Abbs was good enough to let me have some of his magnificent guppies that were both large and highly colorful. The males he gave me were large and brilliant; the females were large and gray; both had black eyes. From my new stock of guppies I noticed that every once in a while an albino guppy, one with pink eyes, appeared. Under the microscope the *albino* has no melanin pigment in its skin or in its eyes. When I selected a few albino guppies and mated them together, they bred true to type.

A mutational change must have occurred among the guppies. This changed one of the genes of the ordinary color effect—the gray type (let us call it *A*)—to the *albino* (a). Then a male gray guppy having one *albino* gene, *Aa*, must have mated at random with a female gray guppy also having one *albino* gene, *Aa*. The way in which some of their offspring showed up as albino guppies may be visualized by the chance union of the albino gene, *a*, in an ovum and a similar albino gene, *a*, in a sperm.

Ovum of a Gray Female

		A	*a*
Sperm of a Gray Male	*A*	1. *AA* Gray	3. *Aa* Gray
	a	2. *Aa* Gray	4. *aa* Albino

The history of the appearance of albinism, its disappearance in the first generation and reappearance in the second, may be illustrated in an accompanying chart. An albino guppy when mated with a wild-type (P₁) produced all wild-type *(Aa)* offspring (no albinos) in the first genera-

Reversion of Fancy Guppies to Wild Coloration

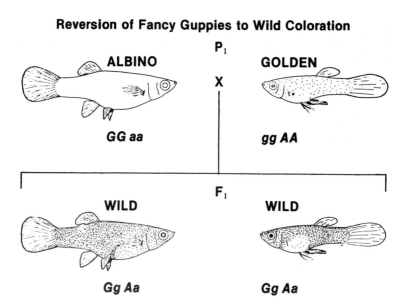

When two fancy varieties, each of which is recessive to the wild type, are mated together, all their offspring have wild coloration. This is because each variety is recessive for only *one* hereditary factor. In this example the golden male is recessive for the golden factor *gg*, but it is dominant with respect to the albino factor *AA*. Thus the golden male genetically is *gg AA*.

tion (F_1). If two wild-type *(Aa x Aa)* members are bred brother to sister, they theoretically produce in the second generation (F_2) three times as many wild-type guppies *(AA, Aa, Aa)* as albinos *(aa)*.

REVERSION TO WILD COLORATION

When two fancy varieties, each of which is recessive to the wild-type, like *golden* and *albino*, are mated together, as is indicated in the chart, all their offspring take on the *wild coloration* of their ancestors. This is because each of the fancy varieties is recessive for only *one* hereditary factor. When combined, the two traits complement each other and produce wild coloring in the offspring.

For example, the golden male guppy is recessive for the golden factor, *gg*, but it is dominant with respect to the al-

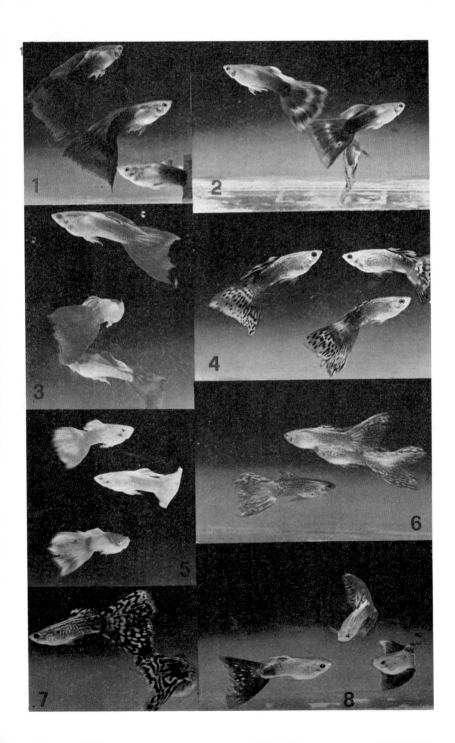

(1) A variety of color types are shown in this assemblage of winners from a Singapore guppy show held during the 1970's; numbers 3, 5 and 8, for example, are albinos. Photos courtesy of the Singapore Guppy Club. (2) A nearly perfect blue delta-tail. The angle of the upper and lower edges of the caudal fin is about 60 degrees, as it should be. Photo by G. Gellrich. (3) Two well matched black delta-tails. Their only fault is the light-colored dorsal fin. Photo by Midge Hill.

Albinism has been capitalized upon in other livebearers besides guppies. Albino swordtails may be even more popular than albino guppies. Photo by H. Hansen, Aquarium Berlin.

bino factor, *AA*. Thus the golden male, genetically, is actually *gg AA*. The albino female, on the other hand, is recessive for the color factor albinism, *aa;* at the same time the albino is dominant for the golden factor, *GG*. Thus the albino female guppy, genetically, is *GG aa*. The albino is prevented from showing its dominant golden trait because the albino gene *aa* inhibits the production of all black or melanin pigmentation even though *GG* is present.

When a golden *(gg AA)* is crossed with an albino *(GG aa)* guppy, all their offspring are wild gray because the offspring have both dominant factors characteristic of the wild guppy *(Gg Aa)*.

Suppose a guppy fancier wants to develop a stock of albinos and all he can secure is a single albino guppy. He might choose to mate it to a *golden* or a *blond* guppy since these light color variants most closely resemble the *albino*.

Golden coloration has been established for many years in livebearers such as platies. The gold female (above) has been a popular strain since the early days of the aquarium hobby. Photo by R. Zukal.

If the fancier knows no principles of inheritance, he is likely to be greatly disappointed when he obtains broods and finds that all of the offspring of the first generation are of the common wild gray coloring. In his disappointment he may discard all of them, thinking they are worthless; not so.

All he need do to obtain a pure line of albinos is to take the gray members of the first generation he has reared to maturity and mate them together, that is, brother to sister. Even though the parents were gray, in the next generation (F_2) he will definitely obtain some albino guppies among the offspring. From these albino guppies he may proceed to build up his stock of albinos with complete assurance that they will not revert to any other type. They cannot revert because (excepting the occurrence of a rare reverse mutation to the wild-type, which is most unlikely) the albinos will always breed true.

An assortment of prize-winning guppies. (1) A half-black delta-tail. This was a second-prize winner, probably because of the small tail. (2) This second-place veil-tail gold has a good dorsal fin, but the caudal fin is too narrow. (3) A fine specimen of a half-black delta-tail. This was the first-place winner. (4) A first-place red delta-tail. (5) The tail on this guppy is a bit small for a delta-tail. This is a delta-tail blue that took first place. All of these fish were entries in a recent German guppy show. Photos by Dr. Karl Knaack.

ZEBRINUS, A BARRED PATTERN

Long before the *golden, blond* and *albino* color varieties of the guppy were discovered, more than 25 other inherited patterns in this small fish had already been described by European geneticists.

The *zebrinus* guppy, as the name implies, is a zebra or barred pattern of 2 to 5 vertical dark pigmented stripes on the caudal peduncle area of the body, that is, between the anal and tail fin. Like so many color patterns in the guppy, *zebrinus* is expressed only in the males but, as we shall see, the females, although unable to express the pattern, are able nevertheless to transmit the hereditary factor for *zebrinus* to their sons.

A trait like *zebrinus*, the gene for which may be carried by both sexes but expressed only in one sex, is known as a sex-limited trait. (Please note that I did not say that the gene or hereditary unit was *sex-linked*—that is something different and definitely does not apply to *zebrinus*.)

Winge mated a *zebrinus* male to several females from a stock known not to carry that marking. He obtained 37 males in the first generation (F_1), all of which showed the *zebrinus* pattern of their father. The F_1 females did not show any pattern. When, however, Winge mated one of the plain F_1 females to a non-*zebrinus* male from a different stock, he obtained 24 guppy males with *zebrinus* coloring and 25 without the pattern. This is just what one would expect, for this represents a back-cross ratio of 1 to 1.

This experiment not only proves that a female may carry a dominant gene like *zebrinus* for a particular pattern without visibly showing it, but it also proves that the female guppy is important in transmitting characters to her offspring.

SELECTIVE BREEDING OF GUPPIES

On page one of his 750-page, fact-filled book *Breeding and Improvement of Farm Animals* (McGraw-Hill), Victor Ar-

Solid color in the dorsal and caudal fins is one of the qualities that the breeders of show guppies strive for. Photo by Dr. Herbert R. Axelrod.

thur Rice says that Americans husband 900 million farm animals, in addition to inestimable numbers of cats and dogs, rodents, rabbits and guinea pigs, foxes, ferrets and mink, goldfish and guppies. Whether the animals are cattle, chickens or guppies each breeder strives to mold his mammal, bird or fish to a certain personal preconceived ideal. The ideal conception may represent commercially valuable combinations of traits or the ideal may be equated with just beauty of color or form or a harmonious combination of these features.

Some guppy fanciers are happy with the ideal of breeding a large fish with a large streamer tail and pennant-like dorsal fin. This type of fancier may disregard uniformity of color pattern. Other breeders may strive to attain consistency in guppies for a certain color pattern. Still others may specialize in a particular shaping of the tail fin, breeding for a lyre-tail, delta-tail, lower sword or some other distinctive form.

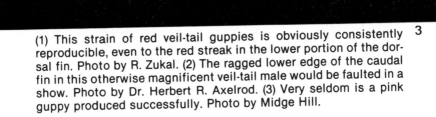

(1) This strain of red veil-tail guppies is obviously consistently reproducible, even to the red streak in the lower portion of the dorsal fin. Photo by R. Zukal. (2) The ragged lower edge of the caudal fin in this otherwise magnificent veil-tail male would be faulted in a show. Photo by Dr. Herbert R. Axelrod. (3) Very seldom is a pink guppy produced successfully. Photo by Midge Hill.

How do they go about it? What is their system of breeding? What about selective breeding, line-breeding, inbreeding, out-breeding and cross-breeding?

You do not have to study Dr. Rice's 750-page book to breed guppies of your choice, but the chances are that you would be a better guppy fancier if you did. The size and type of enclosure, diet and other environmental conditions for breeding dairy cattle are, of course, different from those required for the guppy, but the principles of heredity that apply to both creatures are the same.

Let's not fool ourselves. In order to practice the selective breeding of guppies successfully, a large number of containers are necessary. Assuming the breeder has the essential equipment, his success will depend upon his artistic skill in selecting the type of guppy that most closely approaches his preconceived image of what he wants to create.

In a sense the breeder is like the sculptor who chips a crude block of marble to the likeness that exists only in his imagination. The breeder's task is more difficult than the sculptor's because his ability to create a new form depends upon many unknown factors such as hereditary potential of the male and, even more, the formidable unknown potential of the female guppy.

MATING SYSTEMS AND RECORDS

After a fancier has mated his chosen pair of guppies, he gives their offspring special attention since they will be used to carry on the desired line. Some breeders isolate each young fish after three weeks to one month in a separate container in order to ensure the virginity of the young females. Right here the number of containers the breeder can afford to maintain is one of the limiting factors that may determine success or failure.

If the isolated young guppy turns out to be a male (the signs of maleness lie in the thickening of the anal fin which eventually transforms into the male gonopodium), he and those like him may be combined in a common aquarium but they must not be crowded. Those that develop maleness early are often the more desirable ones—but not always.

If the father of the brood is still vigorous and represents the type the breeder desires to propagate, then the father may be mated back to one or more of his daughters. Winge, the Copenhagen geneticist, successfully back-crossed a guppy male to its daughter, then to one of its granddaughters and finally to a great-granddaughter. Of course, this is not always possible.

Let us go back to the original mating in order to describe one system of recording the results. Some pedigree record is essential in any determined effort to create and maintain good breeding stock. Let us assume the fancier has selected the best pair he can afford. The female parent's number is 1; the male parent's is 2. The pedigree number assigned to all their first generation offspring, male and female, is 3, that is, 1 X 2 = 3 (X in this case representing "by," not "times").

Let us assume the original male (No. 2) is vigorous and he is mated to four of his daughters, the method of recording the pedigree of each of their offspring is as follows:

Female	Male	Pedigree Number of F₁ Offspring
3-1 X	2	No. 4
3-2 X	2	No. 5
3-3 X	2	No. 6
3-4 X	2	No. 7

All the young bearing a distinct pedigree must be reared separately; that is, 4 from 5, 6, and 7; 5 from 6 and 7; and 6 from 7. Again the task of isolating and rearing the young as indicated from the first mating 1 X 2 = 3 must be repeated.

Let us assume that the original male (No. 2) becomes useless as a breeder. By this time the males from pedigree 3

¹ (1) These male and female guppies are close to each other in colora-
tion, but they are not quite close enough for the top prize in the Rus-
sian competition in which they were entered. Photo by H. Kyselov.
(2) Although this guppy might make a good breeder because of its
uniform black color, its ragged caudal fin will keep it out of most
competitions. Photo by Dr. K. Knaack. (3) This guppy has an ex-
cellently formed dorsal fin, but it doesn't match the color of the
caudal fin, an undesirable trait in show guppies. Photo by Dr. K.
Knaack. (4) The bright red color in the dorsal fin of this male is very
unusual, but it does not match the caudal fin very closely. Photo by
Dr. Herbert R. Axelrod.

2

3

4

may be evaluated and one or more chosen to be mated with their sisters, also of pedigree 3.

This kind of mating may be recorded as follows: 3-5 X 3-11 (male individual numbers may start with 11). Their offspring may be given the next available pedigree number which is No. 8, that is 3-5 X 3-11 = No. 8.

To utilize the pedigrees to the best advantage a two card system is recommended, one being a sort of index to the other. The *index* series and the *performance* series are usually put on ruled note cards. The index card will look like this for the matings we have covered so far.

Female	X	Male	Traits of Parents Size, Color, Tail	Pedigree Number of Offspring
1	X	2		3
3-1	X	2		4
3-2	X	2		5
3-3	X	2		6
3-4	X	2		7
3-5	X	3-11		8

The *performance* card represents all the offspring from a given mating. It looks like this beginning with number 1, which is the original female:

1. Describe from whom purchased   (Upper Right Corner)
No. 1
2. From what special stock
3. Characteristics of that stock
4. Size, age, etc.

The pedigree chart for the performance of the offspring of mating between female No. 1 and male No. 2 will look something like this:

1st brood born, date   1   X   2   3
1st male appeared, date
Describe the number of various types

As an example of a pedigree card describing the frequencies of various types of tails obtained by a guppy, let us use the information kindly provided by William H. Hildemann.

Female From Top Sword Stock		Male Double Sword		F_1 Offspring Pedigree
29-1	X	29-1	=	30

Male Offspring (F_1):

Double-swords	61
Top-swords	3
Bottom-swords	2
Oval tails (plain)	2

When Hildemann mated a female of the brood (pedigree 30) to its double-sword brother (pedigree 30), he got the following:

Female		Male Double Sword		F_2 Generation Pedigree
30-1	X	30-11	=	31

Male Offspring (F_2):

Double-swords	18
Top-swords	3

In any effective system of mating, the breeder practices a degree of in-breeding. *In-breeding* may be quite close or not. Close in-breeding involves a mating between a father and his daughter, a mother and her son, or a brother and his sister. *Line-breeding* involves matings between a half brother and a sister or between cousins.

In-breeding is more effective in establishing individual strains—but there are dangers involved with regard to vigor of the offspring. This may be avoided by selecting only in-bred individuals as breeders that show both vigor and the desired traits according to the blueprint in the mind of the fancier. In the choice of the most vigorous breeders it is important to remember that all the fish must be reared under uniform conditions. Otherwise the selection of the most vigorous fish may not represent inherited vigor, which is wanted, but only acquired or apparent vigor, which is not.

GUPPIES